The
Marriage
You
Want

STUDY GUIDE

The Marriage You Want

WANT You

STUDY GUIDE

Moving beyond Stereotypes for a Relationship
Built on Scripture, New Data, and Emotional Health

SHEILA WRAY GREGOIRE
AND DR. KEITH GREGOIRE

WITH BECKY CASTLE MILLER

BakerBooks

a division of Baker Publishing Group
Grand Rapids, Michigan

© 2025 by Sheila Wray Gregoire and Keith R. Gregoire

Published by Baker Books
a division of Baker Publishing Group
Grand Rapids, Michigan
BakerBooks.com

Printed in the United States of America

Library of Congress Cataloging-in-Publication Data
Names: Gregoire, Sheila Wray, 1970– author. | Gregoire, Keith, 1969– author.
Title: The marriage you want study guide : moving beyond stereotypes for a relationship built on scripture, new data, and emotional health / Sheila Wray Gregoire and Dr. Keith Gregoire.
Description: Grand Rapids, Michigan : Baker Books, a division of Baker Publishing Group, [2025] | Includes bibliographical references.
Identifiers: LCCN 2024033541 | ISBN 9781540903983 (paper) | ISBN 9781493449170 (ebook)
Subjects: LCSH: Marriage—Religious aspects—Christianity.
Classification: LCC BV835 .G739 2025 | DDC 248.8/44—dc23/eng/20240814
LC record available at https://lccn.loc.gov/2024033541

Study guide written by Becky Castle Miller, based on and with material from *The Marriage You Want* by Sheila Wray Gregoire and Dr. Keith Gregoire.

Cover design by Kat Lynch.

Baker Publishing Group publications use paper produced from sustainable forestry practices and postconsumer waste whenever possible.

25 26 27 28 29 30 31   7 6 5 4 3 2 1

Contents

How to Use This Book

Welcome to the study guide for *The Marriage You Want*. We created this companion study guide for four audiences and purposes:

for individuals processing the material,

for married couples to improve their relationship,

for premarried couples to set up their marriage for success, and

for small groups of couples to grow in community and support one another as they work through this material.

Each lesson starts with a recap of the highlights from the corresponding chapter in the book. Read these through to reinforce the major ideas from the chapter. The learning goal tells you the outcome you'll work toward in that lesson.

Next are questions for study and reflection, which give you the chance to look back at the chapter to ensure you understand the main concepts while giving you a jumping-off point to start your discussion of the chapter.

Then come questions to help **married couples** dig deeper into the ways the chapter intersects with their relationship and address the issues the chapter brought to the surface for them. Engaged couples are welcome to use these questions, too, where they're appropriate.

A separate set of questions for **premarried couples** helps them apply the ideas from the chapter to their future marriage as well as their present dating or engaged relationship.

A journal prompt then gives each of you a chance to spend a little longer in private considering one of the questions raised by the chapter. If you're working through this study as a couple, consider using a new journal or notebook for each of you to do these journaling exercises.

We've also offered suggestions for prayer together as a couple, because engaging God while working through this material will help strengthen the spiritual side of your relationship.

But it's important to have fun together too! So, in each lesson we suggest a date idea based on the topic of the chapter.

Finally, there is space for you to write down your takeaways—things you most want to remember from the lesson—and action steps. What commitments toward action are you making to each other as you finish each lesson?

Deep discussion with your partner on conflict-heavy topics can cause reactivity and discomfort, so each lesson also includes a self-soothing skill box. These skills, drawn from research primarily in counseling psychology, will help you develop the resilience and calming abilities necessary to engage in hard conversations. Learning and practicing these skills will develop your emotional intelligence and relational maturity, which will serve you and your relationship well in the future, beyond this study guide.

 A Note for Small Group Leaders

We've included in each lesson a set of questions for small groups, Sunday school classes, or Bible study groups to discuss together. These will work best if each couple in the group has done their individual homework for the week first, then comes together to talk and pray with their group. These groups can provide important support and community for couples engaging this important but challenging work.

The group should make a verbal commitment to one another at the outset affirming that they will hold each other's confidences and not share anything outside of the group that has been discussed in the group.

Group leaders will need to set expectations at the start for the kind of discussion appropriate for the group and reiterate them throughout the meetings. Examples of expectations could include:

- Share your own struggles, not your spouse's.
- Do not share graphic sexual details from your relationship.

- Share honestly, but do not make fun of your spouse or endlessly complain about them.
- Do not share anything your spouse would like to keep private.
- If there is a concerning issue about your marriage that your spouse doesn't feel comfortable raising in the group, then find a mentor or therapist that you can raise it with. Please get help if you need it.

Group leaders might hear details of a couple's relationship that raise red flags for abuse. Do not point these out in the group meeting, and do not bring these concerns to both members of the couple since this could make any abuse worse. Consider carefully and privately mentioning your concerns to the partner you fear may be a victim. We strongly recommend that group leaders familiarize themselves with the anti-abuse resources in the appendix of *The Marriage You Want*.

A Note for Married Couples

Reading the material in the book is wonderful if understanding more about what makes a great marriage is your goal. But if actually achieving the marriage you want is your goal, then reading isn't enough. Please do the exercises. Carve out regular time to talk through them and do the date nights. Put the things you're learning into practice!

If one of you realizes during the course of this study that your partner is harmful or destructive, see the appendix at the end of *The Marriage You Want* for resources to learn more about abuse. Abuse is not a marriage problem that the abuse victim can fix, and if that is your story, we hope that this study (and the book) helps you clarify a safe way forward.

A Note for Premarried Couples (and Their Mentors)

We're so glad you're investing the time in your relationship before the wedding! We've got additional questions just for you! We invite you to also participate in the journal prompts, date night activities, prayers, and questions for married couples that are pertinent for you now. We've used the word *spouse* in the activities because it's easier, but feel free to insert fiancé or fiancée where appropriate.

If you are a pastor or a mentor working through this material with an engaged couple as part of their premarital counseling, feel free to assign a few of the questions from the "Married Couples" sections along with the premarital questions. And make sure the couple does their homework!

Premarital preparation time can help you determine whether you two are truly a good fit with each other. We hope this study guide will prepare you for a joyful, healthy married life, whether that is with your current partner or, if you realize they are not right for you, with someone else in the future. If you find through the course of this study guide that you are not well suited as lifelong teammates, you may want to consider postponing or canceling the wedding. Particularly if you discover deep-seated entitlement or abusive tendencies in your partner, seriously heed those red flags. But if this study shows you green flags galore, then celebrate—and commit to putting the things you learn into practice throughout your life together.

Balance

Affection

Responsibility

Emotional
Connection

CHAPTER ONE

The Unity You Want

Chapter Highlights

When Sheila and Keith were in premarital counseling, their pastor showed them a triangle diagram that illustrated how they could grow closer to God and to each other throughout their marriage. This chapter examines four issues that can stretch this triangle out of shape.

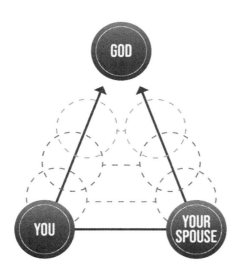

Issue 1: One-size-fits-all gender stereotypes. God calls individuals and God calls couples, and the opportunity God gives each couple to impact the world is as unique as the people in the marriage. Gendered marriage role stereotypes can make people try to become someone they aren't. When each couple, and each spouse, embraces their unique gifts and callings, they can serve God in a unique way, not as stereotypes.

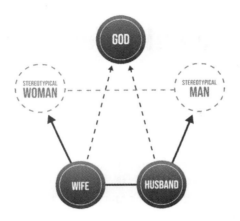

Issue 2: Not loving yourself as well as loving your spouse. The needs of each person in a couple matter. Don't abandon yourself or abandon your spouse and focus only on yourself. Finding balance in meeting each other's needs keeps the triangle in shape.

Issue 3: Tiebreaker husbands. When a husband acts like the authority in the marriage, the couple is more likely to divorce. When men share power with their wives, their marriages are healthier. Wrestling with decisions and making them together is important work that gets short-circuited with the tiebreaker belief. Having a tiebreaker spouse also leads to decreased sexual satisfaction for the non-decision-making spouse. The positive traits of teamwork, partnership, and being heard grow from shared decision-making.

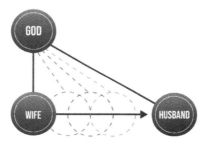

Issue 4: One-sided commitment to safety and marriage growth. When one partner does not want to improve the marriage or is hurting the other, the triangle is distorted. You cannot make your spouse move closer to God or closer to you; you cannot make your spouse change harmful behaviors. Both people in the couple have to be committed to personal health and marriage health to make a marriage work.

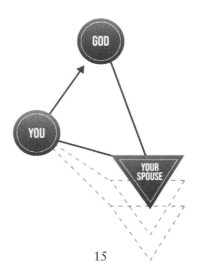

15

Learning Goal

At the end of this lesson, both spouses should have a clearer idea of which of the four triangle-distorting messages are at work in their marriage.

Self-Soothing Skill: Breathwork

Discussing marriage issues can create stress responses in our bodies. We may feel symptoms like increased heart rate, faster or shallower breathing, racing thoughts, panic, a desire to shut down or move away, or defensiveness. In conflict, the activation of our sympathetic nervous system, sometimes called the fight-or-flight response, can make it difficult to regulate our emotions and wisely choose our words.

One tool to restore calm to our nervous system is deep, relaxed breathing. Deep breathing that involves the diaphragm sparks the activation of the parasympathetic nervous system, which calms down the distress response and replaces it with the relaxation response.

Practice deep, relaxed breathing with each other as you begin this session. Box breathing is one way to do deep breathing. Sit in a relaxed posture with both feet on the floor. Put both hands under your legs or fist your hands and put them on your hips. Breathe in, making sure to inflate your stomach, not your lungs, so your stomach presses up against your diaphragm. Imagine a square (or box): each of the four sides represents a four-count. Breathe in for four seconds, hold for four seconds, breathe out for four seconds, hold for four seconds. Set a timer for five minutes and practice breathing together.

Any time during the lesson that you feel reactive or uncomfortable, take a break for some deep breathing. It takes at least forty-five seconds of deep breathing to have an impact on your symptoms. Notice your heart slowing down and your feelings of panic subsiding. As your body calms, notice your emotions and thoughts slowing down as well.

Ideas from: Babatunde Aideyan, Gina C. Martin, and Eric T. Beeson, "A Practitioner's Guide to Breathwork in Clinical Mental Health Counseling," *Journal of Mental Health Counseling* 42, no. 1 (January 2020): 78–94, https://doi.org/10.17744/mehc.42.1.06.

Questions for Study and Reflection

Explain overlapping bell curves in your own words.

How can understanding overlapping bell curves help you think differently about assumptions concerning women and men?

List the three types of people who usually read Christian marriage books.

Which category fits you? Or is there another category you would put yourself in?

What are the four issues that can make the marriage triangle unbalanced?

Questions for Discussion

Married Couples

What gender stereotypes did you have in mind before you got married?

Her answer: _____

His answer: _____

What were your expectations of the roles each of you should and would take on once married?

Her answer: _____

His answer: _____

How do each of you feel your needs are prioritized in your relationship? (1 is "not at all," and 10 is "my needs are fully valued and met.")

Her answer: My needs matter as much as my spouse's needs.

      1   2   3   4   5   6   7   8   9   10

His answer: My needs matter as much as my spouse's needs.

      1   2   3   4   5   6   7   8   9   10

What is a need that you haven't expressed to your spouse before?

Her answer: _____

His answer: _____

Which is *most undesirable* for you: to feel alone, unloved, inadequate, or disrespected?

Her answer: _____

His answer: _____

Which is *most tolerable* for you: to feel alone, unloved, inadequate, or disrespected?

Her answer: _____

His answer: _____

Throughout the book, statistician Joanna Sawatsky uses different scales of marital satisfaction. One of them is the Couples Satisfaction Index, which lists different words for how you might describe your marriage.

On a scale of 1–10, how applicable do you feel each word is to your relationship right now? (1 is least applicable, and 10 is most applicable.)

	Enjoyable	Friendly	Full	Good	Hopeful	Interesting	Sturdy
Her answer:	_____	_____	_____	_____	_____	_____	_____
His answer:	_____	_____	_____	_____	_____	_____	_____

We treat our spouse as we would want to be treated, and we live a life of service within our marriage.

19

Rate how much time and energy you're willing to devote to personal growth and improving your marriage. (1 is "none at all," and 10 is "this is my main priority right now.")

Her answer:

    1   2   3   4   5   6   7   8   9   10

His answer:

    1   2   3   4   5   6   7   8   9   10

How comfortable are you addressing personal growth and relationship issues? (1 is "not at all comfortable," and 10 is "very excited to get started.")

Her answer:

    1   2   3   4   5   6   7   8   9   10

His answer:

    1   2   3   4   5   6   7   8   9   10

If you each scored these last two questions very differently, how do you want to handle that during this study?

Write out your commitment to your spouse during this study. What do you want to promise them about your involvement in this growth process?

Her answer: _____

His answer: _____

Draw a triangle that best represents your marriage as it is now:

Which triangle-distorting message seems to be the biggest issue in your marriage?

What do you as a couple want to do this week to work on this issue?

Premarried Couples

What gender stereotypes come to mind when you think about your future marriage?

Her answer: _____

His answer: _____

What are your expectations of the roles each of you should and will take on once married?

Her answer: _____

His answer: _____

Are there gender stereotypes that are present in your or your partner's family of origin that you do not want to repeat? How will you make plans to address this?

Her answer: _____

_____

His answer: _____

_____

 Journal Prompt

Write about a time when your spouse "outvoted" you and it hurt you. What happened? How did you react? How did you feel? Did you bring up your emotions to your spouse? How did they respond? What, if anything, was the resolution of the conflict?

  Prayer Activity

Go for a prayer walk together. Take turns praying out loud, thanking God for your spouse's unique gifts. Ask God to show you together what unique calling and purpose God has for each of you individually and for you together as a couple. Spend time walking in silence, being open to hearing from God. After your walk, share any encouraging ideas that came to mind during your prayer time.

Date Idea

Celebrate the uniqueness of you as a couple! Plan a date to go somewhere that you both love, even if it's not a typical date location. Pick a place or an activity that reflects your particular interests or skills. For example, a small museum about a special interest, a specialty store for hobby items, a lecture on a college campus about an interesting topic. On your date, each person can share what they think is special and different about themselves. What sets each of you apart from other people? What makes your relationship different from other couples'?

 ## Small Group Discussion Questions

1. Describe the kind of marriage you want. How and when would you interact throughout the day? How would this kind of marriage make you feel?
2. What do you think "good fruit" looks like in marriage?
3. How does this book differ from other marriage books you have studied?
4. What surprised you in reading this chapter?
5. What was a light-bulb moment for you during your discussions with your spouse?
6. If you've already been on your date, talk about what you did and what you learned about each other.
7. Share (anonymously and respectfully) about times you have seen in other marriages one of the four issues that distorts the triangle.
8. Share about times you have seen healthy marriages where both spouses seemed to be moving closer to God and to each other. What are some practical things they did to accomplish this?
9. What was convicting to you in reading this chapter? Did you recognize anything you want to work on in yourself? (Share for yourself and not for your spouse.)
10. How can this community support you and your marriage during this study?

Key Takeaways

-

-

-

-

Action Items

Use this space to list things you want to change or work on, tasks you commit to accomplishing, or follow-up conversations that are needed.

Her answer:

-

-

-

His answer:

-

-

-

Attaching male and female labels doesn't provide any additional help when the stereotypes fit and adds tremendous confusion when they don't.

CHAPTER TWO

The Teamwork You Want

Chapter Highlights

This book doesn't offer one-size-fits-all answers. Advice that works wonders in one situation could cause harm in another. Instead, the authors are offering guiding principles about marriage that can be applied flexibly in different marriages. Learning to apply such guiding principles develops discernment.

Compromise can be a cheap quick-fix. In the story of Gabriella and Brad (see "Teamwork and Compromise Don't Always Go Together" in chap. 2), the pastor tells them to compromise: Brad should help more with the kids, and Gabriella should make herself more available sexually to Brad. The problem with this "compromise" is that the two spouses were not starting from an equal plane.

When approaching marriage problems, it's important to distinguish between *foundation* and *frills*. Which marriage issues are "rocks" (foundational to marital health) and which are "gravel" (frills for extra enjoyment)?

The needs in a marriage can be visualized in another triangle analogy, a pyramid-shaped need hierarchy.

The base layer is *surviving*, in which a couple is focused on life basics: food, shelter, bills, parenting. Couples in this tier are doing the bare minimum of being good roommates to each other. The middle tier is *living*, where a couple can advance to enjoying life—building the relationship, enjoying sex, pursuing comfort. The top tier is *thriving*, where both members of a couple have space for self-actualization and pursuing their passions. Both members of the couple should be on the same tier at the same time

MARRIAGE HIERARCHY OF NEEDS

or the relationship will be unbalanced. The marriage can only advance as high as the member at the lowest level.

Entitlement is one spouse thinking they deserve to live at a higher tier than their spouse or that they deserve a frill that costs their spouse something foundational. They push their spouse to a lower tier while they enjoy a higher one (as Brad did with Gabriella). The antidote to entitlement is teamwork. A team approach in marriage focuses on both spouses working on the foundational needs first so that together they will then be able to both experience the frills.

Learning Goal

At the end of this lesson, both spouses should be able to identify where their marriage is on the hierarchy of needs (surviving, living, or thriving) and notice where one or both of them is feeling entitled.

Self-Soothing Skill: Distress Tolerance

Confronting uncomfortable truths about ourselves, our spouses, and our marriages can be distressing. These sensations can overwhelm us and cause us to want to shut down and avoid talking about the problem. If we want to grow in marital health, we need to increase our ability to handle this discomfort.

Distress tolerance refers to a person's ability to handle difficult emotional or physical states and experiences. People have different natural capacities for handling distress based on their disposition, personality, self-regulation skills, and life experiences. However, distress tolerance can be learned and increased. People who struggle to tolerate distress may respond poorly when stressed or uncomfortable by avoiding the discomfort or reacting in extreme ways.

A person's ability to cope with distress is impacted by their ability to regulate themselves, appraise their emotions, and manage their behavior. People with anxiety disorders, trauma disorders, and ADHD or autism may struggle more with distress tolerance.

The first step to increasing your distress tolerance is to become aware of your own capacity as it stands right now and to evaluate your current go-to responses. Consider these questions:

How do I cope with uncertainty?
How do I cope with ambiguity?
How do I cope with frustration?
How do I cope with uncomfortable emotions?
How do I cope with uncomfortable physical sensations?

The next step is to notice when you are getting distressed. If a conversation with your spouse is causing you distress, say so out loud. Agree to take a break. During the break, employ self-soothing skills like the breathing exercises from the last lesson. Then re-enter the conversation with your spouse.

Consider using a timer to track how long you can handle the discomfort of a hard conversation. See if you can increase the span by a minute or two each time you have an uncomfortable conversation.

Ideas from: Michael J. Zvolensky, Anka A. Vujanovic, Amit Bernstein, and Teresa Leyro, "Distress Tolerance: Theory, Measurement, and Relations to Psychopathology," *Current Directions in Psychological Science* 19, no. 6 (2010): 406–10, http://www.jstor.org/stable/41038610.

Questions for Study and Reflection

What have you been taught about compromise as it pertains to your marriage?

How has compromise worked or not worked for you as a couple?

Have you ever agreed to a compromise that seemed unfair to one of you? How did you both feel about it?

Describe the difference between foundations and frills.

Teams are only as good
as their weakest member.

What are the three tiers in the marriage hierarchy of needs? Which aspects of marriage go in which tier?

_____

_____

How would you define *entitlement*?

_____

_____

How would you define *teamwork* in marriage?

_____

_____

  ## Questions for Discussion

Married Couples

On which tier of the marriage hierarchy of needs would you place your own experience currently within your marriage? (Circle one.)

Her answer: Surviving   Living   Thriving

His answer: Surviving   Living   Thriving

After evaluating your individual tiers, which tier would you as a couple say your marriage is currently on? (Circle one.)

Her answer: Surviving   Living   Thriving

His answer: Surviving   Living   Thriving

Think of several issues over which you frequently conflict. List them below and categorize them as "foundations" or "frills."

Her answer:

Foundations: _____

Frills: _____

His answer:

Foundations: _____

Frills: _____

Take a moment to dream. If you both individually and your marriage together were at the thriving tier, what might life look like for you? What would you pursue individually and together?

_____

_____

What is one step you can take today that would move your marriage up the hierarchy of needs?

_____

Premarried Couples

Work through the previous questions and identify which tier you think your relationship is currently on. (Circle one.)

Her answer: Surviving   Living   Thriving

His answer: Surviving   Living   Thriving

What are the areas, if any, of your current relationship where you see entitlement at work?

Her answer: _____

His answer: _____

What are your plans for dealing with the surviving-tier issues (income, housing, food, housework, childcare, etc.) once you get married? What problems do you anticipate in these areas?

_____

_____

What will thriving look like for you once you are married? What passions do you want to pursue as a couple and as individuals?

_____

_____

What decisions can you make today to prepare for a thriving marriage? What needs to change in your relationship trajectory?

Her answer: _____

His answer: _____

What healthy compromises might you have to make to support each other's passions?

_____

_____

Journal Prompt

Consider areas in your marriage where *you* might feel entitled. Where have you prioritized your own desires in a way that has cost your spouse?

Consider areas in your marriage where you think your spouse is entitled. Where have your needs been subsumed under your spouse's choices and priorities?

After you have journaled separately, discuss your findings with each other. Try to listen to each other with compassion and without judgment.

Prayer Activity

Spend time praying alone, asking God to show you where you have been selfish or entitled. Listen openly for any uncomfortable revelations about yourself. After you have prayed alone, come together and confess to each other any areas where you have put your desires above theirs.

Date Idea

Identify one dream or passion you have as a couple. What is something you can do that would help you both thrive together? Plan a date around that activity. Perhaps you are both passionate about ministry to unhoused people—plan a time to make supply kits and distribute them or plan to volunteer at a shelter. Maybe you both love animals and could volunteer to provide a day of respite care for an animal foster program. If you love decorating your home, pick up a secondhand piece of furniture to refinish together.

Small Group Discussion Questions

In a small group, make sure you are confessing your own sins, not your spouse's! Talking about the ways your spouse has harmed you is important—you do not owe them silent loyalty. But that is usually better accomplished by talking to safe friends or a therapist privately rather than in a group in front of your spouse.

1. Tell the story of a time you have seen a couple manage a truly fair and healthy compromise.
2. What do you think of the way this book defines *entitlement*?
3. If you feel comfortable, share a time you have acted entitled in your marriage.
4. Share where you have discovered you are on the hierarchy of needs.

5. How can this group support your marriage in tangible ways as you move toward thriving?

6. If you are just surviving now, how can this group materially help you get by? For example, can they bring meals, help with childcare, or help with household projects?

7. Tell the group about your dreams as a couple. What do you hope to accomplish in this world together?

8. Read together the Bible passages mentioned in this chapter (Prov. 3:27; 20:23; Matt. 22:39; 1 Cor. 7:32–34; Gal. 6:5; 2 Thess. 3:10). What biblical principles can you gather from these texts to apply to your marriage?

9. What do you want teamwork to look like in your marriage?

Key Takeaways

-
-
-
-

Action Items

Her answer:

-

-

-

His answer:

-

-

-

Entitlement enters a marriage any time one person believes they deserve frills without having to build the foundation.

Balance

Affection

Responsibility

Emotional Connection

CHAPTER THREE

The Friendship You Want

Chapter Highlights

Sea otters hold paws to avoid drifting away from each other while they sleep. Intentional affection can help human couples avoid drifting as well. Investing time to spend with your spouse and showing them you care about them will help cultivate affection.

With busy lives, it can be hard to create that time together. Instead of taking on more work and events, start by rethinking normal life to make natural opportunities to connect. Bundling habits—connecting a new activity to an existing habit or routine—is one way to change daily life. Consider your evening routine: Is there time and space to set up some new habits together? Sharing a bedtime when possible can increase marital satisfaction, but so can setting up other low-key connection opportunities during the day. Doing chores or errands together is one way to increase "low-grade" time together.

Bids for connection are important in building a happy marriage. These are signals one person gives the other that indicate they want to engage. Responding positively to those signals creates a happy connection. Couples in happy marriages have five positive interactions for every one negative interaction.

Laughing and playing together are important, and this will look different for every couple. Couples can try each other's hobbies and make lists of things they enjoy doing together so they have non-screen ideas for recreation. The important thing is to ask each other, "Are we creating memories where we share experiences that matter and where we feel connected?"

Serving in a church together can increase connection and affection, if the church is a safe community. Prayer can bring couples together when they feel distant, and it can make space for vulnerable communication that feels hard or uncomfortable outside of prayer.

Tough life circumstances can make time together hard to find. If the end of a hard season is visible, you can survive the survival season. But if your long-term pace of life is exhausting, consider making some major life changes to create more space for downtime together.

Learning Goal

At the end of this lesson, both spouses should have a better idea of the changes they want to make in their life—short term and long term—to create more space for connection and affection together.

> Don't make things harder than they need to be. Instead, to create more connection, simply rethink how you do normal life.

Self-Soothing Skill: Co-Regulation

Babies and children who are not yet capable of self-regulation need their caregivers to help them regulate their emotions, reactions, and physiological states through co-regulation. While parent-to-child co-regulation is one-sided, with the parent taking responsibility to calm themselves so they can calm their child, adult-to-adult co-regulation can be mutual. Adults have more capacity for self-regulation, but one of the benefits of a romantic partnership is co-regulation. Partners can take turns being the one to regulate the other or can engage in soothing activities that help both of them regulate together.

Co-regulation involves mirror neurons. Humans naturally mimic what they see and hear, so when one person slows their breathing, speaks softly, and moves gently, the person witnessing them will naturally tend to do the same things.

If you or your spouse starts to feel upset or reactive while going through a study guide lesson, it can be a good opportunity for the other partner to help them regulate. The calmer partner in the moment can take the lead on moving into co-regulating activities. Some ideas to try include doing diaphragm breathing exercises together, maintaining eye contact for several minutes, holding each other in a long hug until both bodies relax, speaking kind words in a soft voice, or gently rubbing the other person's arms, back, or legs. The activities will be most successful if the leading partner can keep their own emotions, body responses, and nervous system well-regulated and share that sense of well-being with the more distressed partner.

Leadership in co-regulating should go back and forth between partners. If one person has to do the majority of the work of regulating the other, the relationship is unbalanced and could move into a caregiving relationship instead of an equal partnership. The person who needs more help from a partner to regulate should invest in learning self-regulation skills through the exercises in this workbook and/or with a licensed therapist.

A healthy, well-attached adult partnership has numerous health benefits from co-regulation, including a stronger parasympathetic nervous system response (the aspect of the autonomic nervous system responsible for stopping stress reactions) and lower blood pressure.

Ideas from: David A. Sbarra and Cindy Hazan, "Coregulation, Dysregulation, Self-regulation: An Integrative Analysis and Empirical Agenda for Understanding Adult Attachment, Separation, Loss, and Recovery," *Personality and Social Psychology Review* 12, no. 2 (2008): 141–67, https://doi.org/10.1177/1088868308315702.

Questions for Study and Reflection

What are some reasons people turn to screens during their downtime?

How does habit bundling work?

What are the impacts of nighttime screen usage and a bedtime routine on sleep quality?

How does a shared bedtime impact a marriage relationship?

Explain in your own words how bids for connection work.

Why do you think couples need five positive interactions for every negative one in order to feel connected?

How do a church community and faith impact a marriage relationship?

_____

_____

Questions for Discussion

Married Couples

On a scale of 1–10, if you and your spouse have an hour to drive and chat, how do you feel about your relationship afterward? (1 is very distant and 10 is highly connected.)

Her answer:

1   2   3   4   5   6   7   8   9   10

His answer:

1   2   3   4   5   6   7   8   9   10

What are the top three aspects of your life that keep you from spending more time together?

Her answer: _____

His answer: _____

What activities do each of you tend to turn to for low-demand escapism or entertainment?

Her answer: _____

His answer: _____

List three moments in your day when affection could become a habit.

What is your current evening routine?

How might you be able to alter your nighttime rhythms to spend more low-grade time together (including having a shared bedtime, if possible)?

Which daily life necessities that you do separately could you start doing together? For example, cooking or running errands.

Explain to each other how you commonly express bids for connection. Discuss how you might have missed each other's bids in the past.

Her answer:

_____

_____

His answer:

_____

_____

What activities that you do together actually feel fun to both of you? What makes you laugh together?

What hobbies does one person enjoy that the other could begin to participate in to increase your time together?

Assess honestly: Are you both happy in your current church? Does your church teach healthy messages about marriage? What does an ideal church look like for each of you? Are there opportunities for you each to use your spiritual gifts and passions to serve others? Do you need to consider changing churches to better support your individual and joint spiritual lives?

Who is currently the spiritual leader in your relationship? How might you be able to share the responsibility for spiritual health in your individual and joint lives?

What aspects of your current life exhaust you? What could you change to get more rest and connection? Think small (daily routines) as well as big (career change, moving near family).

Premarried Couples

Make a list of activities you each find fun. Then compare the lists. What might you do together once you are married that you will both find fun and enjoyable?

Her answer: _____

His answer: _____

What kind of church does each of you prefer? Consider tradition, denomination, size, location, doctrinal priorities, service opportunities. When you are married, will one of you join the other's church? Will you find a new church together? What factors will you use to evaluate whether the church is a good fit for you as a couple?

How does each of you like to serve God and God's people? What service opportunities can you pursue together?

What does spiritual connection look like for each of you? How might you like to pursue spiritual growth together?

What are your beliefs about spiritual leadership in marriage? How do they compare or contrast with each other's?

List the factors that might make your future marriage a survival time. What will impact your ability to spend time together regularly? Make plans now to set up a sustainable pace of life for your marriage.

 **Journal Prompt**

Assess the level of connection you have with your spouse. How much time do you spend together having fun, enjoying each other, and growing closer? What would you like to change about this aspect of your life? Dream big—if time, money, and your spouse's interest level were no object, what would you ideally like to do together?

Then assess: What is keeping those dreams from becoming reality?

Prayer Activity

Pray together with a focus on opening up to God emotionally while with your partner. Take turns praying out loud, trying to increase the level of vulnerability with God you share in front of your partner. Discuss afterward. How did it feel? What sensations and thoughts came up during the experience? Was it easier to be open with your spouse when you were being open with God?

Date Idea

Figure out a mundane life activity one or both of you needs to accomplish. Plan a time to do it together, especially if it's something you don't normally do together. Focus on enjoying each other's company during the experience. Add a little treat into the outing—maybe a scoop of ice cream, a short stop at a scenic location, or a few minutes of kissing in the car.

Small Group Discussion Questions

1. Share with the group what you did for your mundane date. What did you discover about each other during the experience?

2. Share your reflections on your individual distress tolerance. How are you handling these potentially uncomfortable discussions? What are you doing to increase your tolerance?

3. Share recommendations of comedians you enjoy. The group leader can compile a list of names shared by the group so each couple has ideas of comedy to watch together to increase laughing together.

4. How are you succeeding in carving out time to spend together, especially if you are in a busy season of life?

5. What are ways you can make it easier to pray together or have spiritual discussions in your marriage? Why is this sometimes difficult?

6. Is there anything practical the group as a community can do to alleviate stress in your life so you can connect better? (Babysit for one another, cook a meal for another couple so they can have an at-home date night, help with a home repair issue, etc.)

7. What are your beliefs about spiritual leadership in marriage? How have they been challenged or confirmed by this chapter?

Key Takeaways

-
-
-
-

Action Items

Her answer:

-
-
-

His answer:

-
-
-

Quality time looks different for each couple.

CHAPTER FOUR

The Passion You Want

Chapter Highlights

Focusing on frequency of sex is *not* the best starting place for fixing your sex life! Instead, focus on the factors that contribute to a healthy sex life, and frequency will tend to take care of itself.

If couples define sex as penis-in-vagina intercourse that results in a man's orgasm, this will likely result in less-than-stellar sex for both people. Sex is meant to be intimate, mutual, and pleasurable for both people.

Intimate

Sex should be a deep knowing where both people feel seen and wanted. The quality of a relationship outside of sex impacts sexual happiness. If sex is not intimate, having sex can actually damage the marriage.

Porn use is a betrayal of your spouse's trust and a form of cheating. It can also inhibit intimacy because it lets people self-soothe in an unhealthy way instead of dealing with the root of their discomfort and learning healthy coping skills. Quitting porn involves dealing with the entitlement to use other people and addressing the wounds and shame for which the person is self-soothing. When getting adjusted to living without porn, it's important not to use a spouse as a porn-replacement tool. Beyond actual porn use, some people develop a pornified style of relating, which treats sex like a transaction or an entitlement.

A history of sexual abuse can impact intimacy in marriage. Therapy can help reveal and heal the traumatic results of sexual abuse.

Pleasurable for Both

While 95% of evangelical men almost always or always reach orgasm in a given sexual encounter, only 48% of evangelical women do, giving us a 47-point orgasm gap. Yet many evangelical resources tell couples to increase sexual frequency without focusing on increasing sexual satisfaction for women. When sex is not pleasurable for a woman, her libido decreases. Sexual stimulation beyond intercourse is usually key for women's pleasure.

Sexual pain is a widespread issue. Evangelical women have higher rates of sexual pain disorders than the general population, largely because they have absorbed toxic messages about sex and had initial sexual experiences that did not focus on their pleasure and often caused them pain. Starting a sexual relationship by focusing on mutual pleasure will increase sexual satisfaction throughout the marriage.

Mutual

Sex is something for both partners to enjoy together, not something that one spouse owes the other. Obligation sex or duty sex can make the marriage worse.

Focusing on the foundation of a good relationship will often resolve or smooth over libido differences and differences in preferences for sexual frequency.

> Prioritize the ingredients
> that make for great sex,
> not the frequency of intercourse.

Learning Goal

At the end of this lesson, both spouses should understand some of the factors that could be contributing to sexual issues in the relationship. They will also consider how to make their sexual relationship intimate, pleasurable, and mutual.

Self-Soothing Skill: Window of Tolerance

The window of tolerance is a way of visualizing your ability to manage daily stress. Picture two parallel lines. When you are within your own unique window of tolerance, you are between the two lines. As you move through the ups and downs of life each day, imagine them as waves within the two lines. When the waves stay within the lines, you can calmly handle the stressors. When the stressors are overwhelming, the waves go beyond the lines. When the waves go above the lines, you may react in hyperaroused ways—disproportionate emotional reactions like rage or weeping, intrusive thoughts, yelling, feeling panic in your body, lashing out at people. When the waves go below the lines, you might react in hypoaroused ways—low mood, numbness, depression, withdrawal from people.

Life factors such as childhood trauma, damaging relationships, illness, or overwhelming current events can shrink your window of tolerance, leaving you feeling unable to cope with stress and difficulty. The good news is that you can learn how to increase the size of your window, and you can learn how to bring yourself back within your window when you notice you are outside it.

Draw two parallel lines to illustrate your window of tolerance. How big is your window?

Draw waves up and down within the lines. What are the waves of daily stressors that take up space in your window? How close do they come to the lines? How much margin do you have between the lines and the waves most days?

Draw a small circle on that diagram to show where you normally find yourself in your window of tolerance in daily life. Are you within the window, or do you usually find yourself above or below the lines?

Begin paying attention to your window of tolerance as you do these study guide exercises with your partner. Do any aspects of this relationship-building work spike you above or below your window?

When you feel yourself moving out of your window of tolerance with heightened or lowered reactions, take a break from the conversations. Try breathing exercises, gentle physical exertion, or soothing practices like a shower or lying down in a dark room. When you feel like you are back within your window, resume the conversation.

Regular self-care, therapy, and daily diaphragm breathing exercises can actually increase your window of tolerance so you can better handle life stress each day.

Ideas from: Abby Hershler, "Window of Tolerance," chapter 4 in *Looking at Trauma: A Tool Kit for Clinicians*, ed. Abby Hershler, Lesley Hughes, Patricia Nguyen, and Shelley Wall (University Park, PA: Penn State University Press, 2021), 25–28, https://doi.org/10.1515/9780271092287-008.

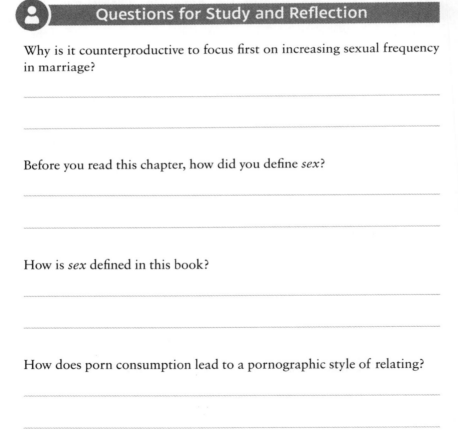

Questions for Study and Reflection

Why is it counterproductive to focus first on increasing sexual frequency in marriage?

Before you read this chapter, how did you define *sex*?

How is *sex* defined in this book?

How does porn consumption lead to a pornographic style of relating?

What are some of the negative associations a person can develop toward sex?

_____

_____

What are some reasons an orgasm gap exists in many Christian marriages?

_____

_____

Why is sexual play outside of just intercourse important in making sex pleasurable and mutual?

_____

_____

How does obligation sex impact a marriage relationship?

_____

_____

Questions for Discussion

Married Couples

How intimate is your current sexual relationship? (1 is "not intimate at all," and 10 is "fulfills all my dreams of intimacy.")

Her answer:

    1   2   3   4   5   6   7   8   9   10

His answer:

    1   2   3   4   5   6   7   8   9   10

How pleasurable is your current sexual relationship? (1 is "actually, it's painful," and 10 is "extremely pleasurable and orgasmic.")

Her answer:

1   2   3   4   5   6   7   8   9   10

His answer:

1   2   3   4   5   6   7   8   9   10

How mutual is your current sexual relationship? (1 is "I only have sex because it's a duty and an obligation," and 10 is "Sex is something we both want, enjoy, and initiate.")

Her answer:

1   2   3   4   5   6   7   8   9   10

His answer:

1   2   3   4   5   6   7   8   9   10

Discuss your sex education experiences. Share with each other what you learned about sex and when. How did this impact your sex life at the beginning of your relationship? How do those lessons still impact you today?

Is your current sexual relationship an accurate reflection of the rest of your relationship? How so?

    Her answer: _____

    His answer: _____

What is the history you have with pornography? Is that something you struggle with?

    Her answer: _____

    His answer: _____

If your partner confesses to using porn, share how you feel about their usage.

Do you notice your partner having a pornified style of relating? What are some of the signs you identify?

If porn is a problem, what steps are you willing to commit to in order to heal the issues driving that behavior?

Do either of you have negative associations with sex or sexual pain? Is there anything in your sexual history that has negatively influenced your view of sex that you want to share with your partner?

Discuss your wedding night or first sexual experience together. What went well? What did not go well? What do you wish you had done differently? How might your initial sexual experiences together still be impacting your sexual relationship today?

How aligned (or unaligned) are your libidos? What factors do you think contribute to the differences?

What do you think you need to do differently to make sex great for both of you?

Let's address frequency last, since addressing it first can cause problems. How often do you tend to have sex now?

How often did you have sex at the start of your sexual relationship?

If the frequencies are different, what has led to the change?

What do you need to do to make your relationship better so that in the future, your sex life can improve?

Premarried Couples

Share about your physical and sexual experiences with any previous partners. Focus on whether those experiences were intimate, pleasurable, and mutual. Were any of those experiences harmful? How do they impact your perspective on sex today? The person who is listening should work to be compassionate and nonjudgmental.

What do you like about the physical affection in your relationship right now? What would you like to be different about it?

What are your expectations for sex in your marriage? What are your hopes?

If either of you is currently consuming porn, what is your plan to grow and heal so you don't bring that maladaptive coping mechanism into your marriage?

If either of you has experienced sexual trauma, what is your plan to pursue trauma counseling to heal those wounds?

How can you plan your honeymoon to create space for emotional intimacy, patience, and mutual pleasure?

 ## Journal Prompt

What are your dreams for sex? You don't need to share this journal entry with your spouse. Give yourself space to consider what the ideal sexual connection would look like for you. How is that different from your current experience? Is there anything you can change to move toward the kind of sexual relationship you want to cultivate?

Prayer Activity

If you feel comfortable, pray with gratitude for the gift of sex and the possibilities for pleasure. Pray for God to help each of you be an intimate, loving, mutually pleasuring sexual partner for your spouse. If pain and difficulty around sex makes that prayer feel impossible, consider praying a lament about how sex has been used to harm you. Make space to grieve the losses that have come from bad sexual experiences. If this lesson has revealed ways you have hurt your spouse, pray a confession in front of them and also apologize directly to them.

Date Idea

If you are both generally happy with sex together, if you feel safe, and if you are confident that both of you will focus on each other's pleasure, discuss your sexual fantasies with each other. What is something you both would like to try that you haven't done before? Carve out plenty of time for a sexual exploration date.

If sex is a struggle for any reason, plan a nonsexual physical date to build your relationship. Play pickleball, go skating, take a yoga class together, book a massage, etc. Whatever you choose, practice the principles from this chapter. Make sure it is an activity you both enthusiastically consent to doing—if one of you has any hesitation about doing it, have an open conversation about consent where everyone's no is respected. Choose something that will allow for intimate connection, that is enjoyable for both of you, and that will ensure you both have a good time. Don't be competitive! Remember the point is mutual pleasure.

> **If sex is an obligation, then sex isn't a knowing; it's an owing.**

Small Group Discussion Questions

Because this topic could bring up people's trauma and deep pain, group leaders should carefully monitor everyone's comfort and safety during the discussion. Let everyone know there is no pressure to answer any question they don't want to answer. Also ensure group members do not overshare.

1. What is the most interesting thing you learned in this chapter?
2. What was your reaction to the sexual statistics in this lesson?
3. How did the advice in this chapter differ from other Christian sexual teaching you have heard?
4. Read 1 Corinthians 7 together (the whole chapter) and discuss. How do verses 3–5 fit into the whole argument of the chapter? Of the book? How can this passage be interpreted in a way that leads to good fruit?
5. What do you wish you had known about sex before you got married?
6. If you have children or young people you care for, what would you tell them about sex before they get married?
7. What kinds of connections in daily life increase your sexual desire for your spouse?
8. Share ideas for emotional regulation and self-soothing so that you don't turn to porn or use your spouse sexually in order to self-soothe. What strategies help you instead?
9. How can we as a group notice and hold one another accountable regarding changing unhealthy views and teaching on sex? For example, what are the signs that someone might have remnants of a pornographic style of relating or might normalize obligation sex?

Key Takeaways

-
-
-
-

Action Items

Her answer:

-
-
-

His answer:

-
-
-

> Start thinking of sex as sexual play
> that you do for each other that brings
> pleasure to each other.

Balance

Affection

Responsibility

Emotional
Connection

CHAPTER FIVE

The Partnership You Want

Chapter Highlights

Sharing housework and mental load significantly contributes to marital satisfaction—more than many of us realize. When each spouse does half the housework, their marital flourishing score is the highest. When one person does almost all the housework alone, their marital flourishing score is the lowest, whether or not that spouse works outside the home.

A woman's relational satisfaction and desire for her spouse goes down over the course of a marriage much more than a man's does. This seems tied to women often doing more of the housework and caregiving than men. Men aren't lazy or incapable, but in our culture, they seem to be able to get away with being a bad teammate more than women can. By looking honestly at the statistics provided in chapter 5, couples can learn to work better toward team making.

Rather than assigning chores based on gender roles, consider each partner's circumstances, gifts, and preferences. As life circumstances change, the responsibilities can change so that each person contributes their fair share. Balancing rest and leisure time is a good place to start establishing fairness. Each partner should get equivalent downtime.

One partner working outside the home does not excuse them from sharing housework when they are home. Even if one spouse stays home with children while the other works, they can still share work and leisure time in the other hours of the day.

"Mental load" is carrying the weight of remembering what needs to be done for each person in the family. That burden should be shared by teammates rather than weighing on one person. The negative dynamic around "nagging" is best dealt with by people following through on their responsibilities rather than attacking the one who is asking for help. Men and women are equally capable of learning to manage mental load.

How can couples create a mental load partnership? Rather than asking your partner for a list, apply your skills to identifying what needs to be done. Eve Rodsky, author of *Fair Play*, recommends owning the whole task from conception to execution. This is more effective for balancing mental load than trying to share different aspects of the same task.

"Weaponized incompetence" is doing a task poorly in order to get out of doing it. Once you take on a task, learn to do it well. Agree together on a minimum acceptable standard for a task, then allow the person who owns the task to take it from there and do it in their own way. If there is an unfair distribution of labor, over time it will weigh on the spouse who carries the heavier load and decrease their marital satisfaction.

Learning Goal

At the end of this lesson, both spouses should have a clear understanding of the teamwork necessary for housework to help both spouses feel satisfied with their marriage. They should also understand mental load and how to share tasks equitably.

A roles-based marriage will tend to be inflexible, while a team approach allows flexibility when circumstances in your relationship change.

Self-Soothing Skill: Progressive Muscle Relaxation

Actively tensing then releasing muscle groups throughout your body can help you feel relaxed. The brain and body stimulation works two ways: your brain tells your body to contract and relax, then the stimulation from the muscles signals the brain. This quickly reduces stress. The results are similar to the relaxation success of deep breathing.

To practice this technique, lie down on a comfortable surface. Move up your body, muscle group by muscle group. Start with your feet. Tighten every muscle in your feet and hold it. Then consciously relax them. Next, do this with your legs, then your core, your chest, your arms, your hands, then your shoulders and neck, and finally, your face. When you are finished, lie still and notice the relaxation in your body.

Ideas from: Loren Toussaint, Quang Anh Nguyen, Claire Roettger, Kiara Dixon, Martin Offenbächer, Niko Kohls, Jameson Hirsch, and Fuschia Sirois, "Effectiveness of Progressive Muscle Relaxation, Deep Breathing, and Guided Imagery in Promoting Psychological and Physiological States of Relaxation," *Evidence-Based Complementary and Alternative Medicine* (July 2021), https://doi.org/10.1155/2021/5924040.

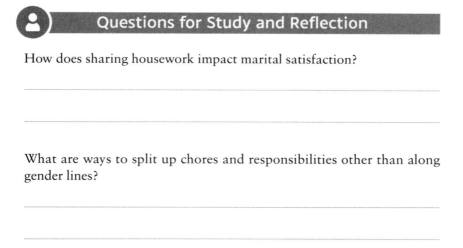

Questions for Study and Reflection

How does sharing housework impact marital satisfaction?

What are ways to split up chores and responsibilities other than along gender lines?

How can couples split housework fairly when one spouse works outside the home and the other doesn't?

Define *mental load* in your own words.

What is *weaponized incompetence?*

Why is it important for couples to balance downtime?

What might be a better word than "nagging" to talk about the dynamic of reminding a spouse to do tasks?

How does dividing up tasks so that one person owns an entire process help with mental load distribution?

Questions for Discussion

Married Couples

How much of the housework do you think you do?

Her answer:

0%   10%   20%   30%   40%   50%   60%   70%   80%   90%   100%

His answer:

0%   10%   20%   30%   40%   50%   60%   70%   80%   90%   100%

How much of the housework do you think your spouse does?

Her answer:

0%   10%   20%   30%   40%   50%   60%   70%   80%   90%   100%

His answer:

0%   10%   20%   30%   40%   50%   60%   70%   80%   90%   100%

Compare and discuss your answers. Discuss any discrepancies in your answers.

How does marital satisfaction correlate with sharing housework in your marriage?

Do you feel resentment about how housework is divided in your home? Try to discuss this in a constructive way, with curiosity and compassion to hear each other instead of becoming defensive.

How much leisure time do each of you have during a normal week to rest, recreate, and have a break from responsibility?

Her answer: _____

His answer: _____

Have you divided housework according to stereotypical gender roles? Was this by choice based on what works best for each of you as individuals, or did you feel forced into those jobs by cultural expectations?

Her answer: _____

His answer: _____

What is your current satisfaction level with the way housework is divided? (1 is totally unsatisfied, and 10 is completely satisfied.)

Her answer:

    1   2   3   4   5   6   7   8   9   10

His answer:

    1   2   3   4   5   6   7   8   9   10

How can you reorganize housework division to better fit your personalities, gifts, schedules, and circumstances? This can always be revised again in the future.

What is your current level of satisfaction with your division of paid work? (1 is totally unsatisfied, and 10 is completely satisfied.)

Her answer:

    1   2   3   4   5   6   7   8   9   10

His answer:

    1   2   3   4   5   6   7   8   9   10

What would it look like to rearrange paid work opportunities for one or both of you? Would you need additional schooling or training? Would you need to move?

Negotiate the working hours for both of you. How can you ensure you both have equal amounts of downtime from housework and paid work?

What is your current satisfaction level with your division of mental load? (1 is totally unsatisfied, and 10 is completely satisfied.)

Her answer:

1   2   3   4   5   6   7   8   9   10

His answer:

1   2   3   4   5   6   7   8   9   10

How can you divide up tasks from conception to execution to evenly divide mental load? Consider reading *Fair Play* to assist with this project.

Discuss the minimum standard of care that each task requires. *How to Keep House While Drowning* by K. C. Davis offers useful advice on practical approaches to care tasks, including how to decide the minimum standard of care.

Premarried Couples

How did your parents divide up housework while you were growing up? What did you like or dislike about their approach?

Her answer: _____

His answer: _____

How do you currently manage housework where you live?

Her answer: _____

His answer: _____

What are your expectations for housework in your marriage?

Her answer: _____

His answer: _____

What are your expectations for paid work in your marriage?

Her answer: _____

His answer: _____

What are the chores you most like to do?

Her answer: _____

His answer: _____

Make a list together of all the tasks you think are important in running a home together and keeping it clean. Then go back through and mark with your initials the favorite or preferred chores for each of you. Circle the chores no one wants to do. How will you divide those?

_____   _____

_____   _____

_____   _____

_____   _____

_____   _____

Considering mental load, which tasks do you want to assign to which partner for your home together, to manage from conception to execution?

_____   _____

_____   _____

_____   _____

What skills will you need to learn to do your assigned tasks well?

Her answer: _____

His answer: _____

Journal Prompt

Think about a task you are responsible for. Write out all the steps to complete the task from conception to execution. Write down all the factors that go through your mind when approaching the task. Get all the details in one place, even if it feels overwhelming. Then read each other's entries and discuss what you learned about how much your partner is carrying with this task.

  Prayer Activity

Take turns praying for your partner regarding their workload, from paid work to housework to childcare. Pray for their success in each area in specific ways.

Date Idea

Take turns planning a surprise date. For each date, one person should be fully responsible for planning all aspects of it. The other person should have no responsibility at all other than showing up. Simply invite your spouse to a day and time and tell them how to dress and assure them that you are taking care of the rest. On your date, discuss who normally plans your dates. How did it feel to be asked on a date you didn't have to plan? How can you share the mental load of dates more in your relationship?

 Small Group Discussion Questions

1. What examples have you seen in movies, books, or TV shows of couples doing well at sharing housework and mental load? What examples have you seen of couples doing it badly?

2. What assumptions did you have coming into marriage about housework / mental load / childcare that your spouse didn't know about? Where did those assumptions come from?

3. What does mental load feel like to you? Share what you're carrying in your mind right now.

4. How does housework currently get divided in your home?

5. How are you planning to change the division of labor to better share the load?

6. Share your dreams for ideal teamwork in your marriage.

7. What skills do you need to develop to do your assigned tasks better?

8. Is there anyone in this group who can help you learn that skill or point you to resources?

Key Takeaways

-
-
-
-

Action Items

Her answer:

-
-
-

His answer:

-
-
-

Children are not a task to divvy up;
children are people who desperately need
a healthy relationship with both parents.

CHAPTER SIX

The Dependability You Want

Chapter Highlights

Taking initiative in a marriage means paying attention to your spouse, deliberately noticing what is going on with them, and taking active steps to make life better or easier for them. Just like an understudy in a theater production, who carefully watches the lead and learns their part so they can step in to play the role in an emergency, a good marriage partner is prepared to help. One way to learn each other's "roles" is to occasionally take care of each other's tasks.

Each spouse needs to take care of their own adult responsibilities, such as making their own medical appointments and caring for their health trajectory—their mental, emotional, and physical health. But if a person has mental illness or neurodivergence, it can be more difficult for that spouse to remember tasks and care for health issues. Education, understanding, and grace are important here. Figure out accommodations and strategies together so that you can be teammates rather than one spouse being a caregiver for the other.

Taking initiative sometimes means learning new skills and growing your capacity to tackle challenges. Sometimes partners can teach each other necessary skills. Other times, one person will need to take action to learn something new.

One area to take initiative is for your own family of origin. Kinkeeping work for extended family should be led by the spouse more closely connected to that family. Setting boundaries with your own parents is also important.

Emotional labor is one job that can't be done by one partner alone. The work of noticing, attuning to, and caring for your family members' emotional health is work each person needs to do to build healthy connections.

Learning Goal

At the end of this lesson, both spouses should be aware of the work they each need to do to take initiative in caring for themselves and for their partner.

Self-Soothing Skill: Working with Your Different "Parts"

One helpful way of understanding our own emotions and motivations is learning about "parts" work. One evidence-based parts work modality is Internal Family Systems (IFS). IFS is a framework for understanding the mind as having multiple "parts," like when a person says, "A part of me would like to hang out with friends, but another part of me wants to go rest at home." All these parts are good and have a protective intent for us, even if they seem to focus on different approaches.

Because these various parts react in current situations to protect us based on past harmful experiences, sometimes their reactions are maladaptive. For example, an inner critic voice might tell us we are failing at our job. The inner critic isn't a pleasant voice, but we can welcome an inner critic part by understanding its purpose—to save us from getting into trouble. We can listen to what it is trying to teach us about our circumstances rather than trying to push it away or silence it. When we listen to our parts with compassion, we can learn their origin and goal. In this case, our inner critic's positive intent is to keep us from getting fired, based on a past experience of losing a job due to a mistake. When we can befriend these parts, we can let go of the past burdens we carry, preventing them from negatively impacting our lives today.

We subconsciously form these protective parts to keep us from re-experiencing a past painful experience. Everyone has many of these protective parts, but everyone also has a Self, the core of their identity, who God made them to be. When Self is present and able to consciously assert itself because it has befriended the protector parts, IFS calls that state Self-Leadership. It's similar to the Christian idea of self-control (Gal. 5:23).

To help you get to know the various reactive, or protector, parts of you, start by noticing the reaction in your body when something happens that upsets or worries you. Where are you feeling that emotion? What kind of sensations are you feeling?

Then focus on the part of yourself that is telling you something. How do you feel toward it? See if you feel any of the following positive traits: compassion, curiosity, clarity, creativity, courage, calm, confidence, and connectedness. Especially if you can engage compassion and curiosity toward the part, move forward with the inner conversation. What is this part trying to protect you from? How long has it been doing this job to try to help you? What is it afraid will happen if it doesn't do this job for you?

Once you have understood where your reaction is coming from, see if you can help this part let go of the burdens it is carrying—the negative beliefs about you or the world that feel too heavy. The more you have these healing internal conversations, the less reactive you will be when hard things happen in your current life.

Ideas from: Richard C. Schwartz and Martha Sweezy, *Internal Family Systems Therapy*, 2nd ed. (New York: Guilford, 2019). For a Christian book about IFS, please see Jenna Riemersma, *Altogether You* (Marietta, GA: Pivotal Press, 2020).

> **Being on the same page regarding in-laws is actually more important than whether the relationships with those in-laws are good.**

Questions for Study and Reflection

What does it mean to take initiative in a marriage?

What does paying attention to your partner's life, interests, and needs communicate to them?

Explain the understudy analogy in your own words.

What aspects of life should each person in a marriage be responsible for personally?

How can couples balance accommodation needs, grace, and personal responsibility?

How can people increase their capacity, and why does that matter?

Explain what *kinkeeping* is and how it works.

Questions for Discussion

Married Couples

Think of a time you were surprised to learn something new about your spouse. What happened?

Her answer:

His answer:

Have you ever gone through a time where one spouse was out of commission? How did the other pick up the slack? What did you learn in that process?

What jobs that your partner is normally responsible for seem like a total mystery to you? What could you do to learn how to handle them yourself?

Her answer: _____

His answer: _____

If one of you lost your job, what would you need to do for the other partner to quickly earn more money? What steps do you need to take now to ensure each of you would be ready to work or change jobs if needed?

Her answer: _____

His answer: _____

Do you have any chronic health problems, mental illnesses, or neurodiversity that impact your ability to take initiative?

What do you wish your partner understood about your particular struggles?

What educational resources can you find that could help educate each other about the things that make life harder for you? Search for some and list them here. What is your plan to pursue this learning?

What could you realistically do to take initiative for the aspects of your struggles that you can control?

How would the specifics of your day-to-day life change if you cultivated more understanding, grace, and compassion toward each other?

How do you divide the labor of making medical and dental appointments? Does that need to change?

Is there an area of life where you need to expand your capacity?

Her answer: _____

His answer: _____

List some ideas for ways you can start taking initiative toward that capacity expansion.

Her answer: _____

His answer: _____

How stressful is money in your marriage? (1 is "it's tearing us apart," and 10 is "we don't struggle at all with money conflict.")

Her answer:

    1   2   3   4   5   6   7   8   9   10

His answer:

    1   2   3   4   5   6   7   8   9   10

What is your current satisfaction level with your relationship with HER parents? (1 is totally unsatisfied, and 10 is completely satisfied.)

Her answer:

    1   2   3   4   5   6   7   8   9   10

His answer:

    1   2   3   4   5   6   7   8   9   10

What is your current satisfaction level with your relationship with HIS parents? (1 is totally unsatisfied, and 10 is completely satisfied.)

Her answer:

1   2   3   4   5   6   7   8   9   10

His answer:

1   2   3   4   5   6   7   8   9   10

If you are not on the same page regarding relationships with each other's parents, what needs to change there?

Who does the kinkeeping work for each family of origin? Does anything about this arrangement need to change? What would that look like in practical ways throughout the next year?

Premarried Couples

How do you currently take initiative in your relationship to anticipate and meet each other's needs and desires?

Her answer: _____

His answer: _____

How do you currently take initiative to care for your own life responsibilities?

Her answer: _____

His answer: _____

As you plan out your division of labor for after you're married, how do you want to prepare to also learn to be each other's understudies?

Her answer: _____

His answer: _____

What struggles in your life hold you back? How can you take initiative to start changing those things for yourself before you enter marriage?

Her answer: _____

His answer: _____

How do you want to divide up the work of making medical and dental appointments for yourselves, any children, and pets?

What do each of you see as the difference between accepting someone as they are and enabling them to never grow?

Her answer: _____

His answer: _____

What struggles do you anticipate needing accommodation and support for after you're married? Discuss honestly now how you can plan to care for each other and take responsibility for yourselves.

 Journal Prompt

Write a journal entry as if you were your spouse. Write about a struggle they have. Try to imagine what it feels like for them. What is their daily experience? What is particularly hard for them? What might they desire to receive from you?

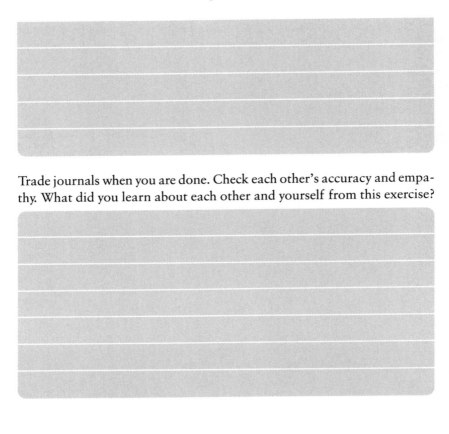

Trade journals when you are done. Check each other's accuracy and empathy. What did you learn about each other and yourself from this exercise?

 Prayer Activity

Pray for your partner regarding a painful aspect of their life. Ask God to strengthen and assist them in specific ways. Let this prayer time develop God's compassion for them in you.

 Date Idea

Tackle tasks you have been procrastinating about that will set you both on a positive trajectory. Consider making appointment phone calls, filing, sorting socks, doing your taxes, planning menus for the month, running errands, answering emails. Play some music and get your favorite snacks to make it more enjoyable. Set a time limit for your work so you know there is an end point in sight. Body doubling (doing a task in the presence of another person, even if they are doing something else) can be a great way to accomplish tasks that seem too hard to do alone.

 ## Small Group Discussion Questions

1. Share with the group something about yourself that they might not know. Use this time to get to understand one another in a more detailed way.

2. Tell about a time your spouse anticipated a need or a want for you and met it. How did that make you feel?

3. Read Ecclesiastes 4:9–10 together. What are some of the benefits of having a team in marriage?

4. When have you taken initiative to change something that was holding you back? What was the result?

5. What are you doing to ensure you have the best possible chance of growing old together? Have you watched other couples grow old together badly? How can you ensure you don't get on the same trajectory?

6. Have you ever had a time when one of you had to act as a caregiver for the other? How did that impact your marriage?

7. As you are comfortable, share things that are difficult for you that this chapter brought up. Did you see yourself in any of the struggles mentioned here?

8. If money is a serious stress point in your marriage, can you share a specific financial need you have? Group members can consider contributing a small amount to meet a few needs for one another to reduce that stress. You could even rotate meeting a need for each of several different couples over the next few group meetings.

Key Takeaways

-

-

-

Action Items

Her answer:

-

-

-

His answer:

-

-

-

Taking initiative to set you and your family up to thrive in the future is a powerful way of loving and caring for your spouse.

Balance
Affection
Responsibility
Emotional Connection

CHAPTER SEVEN

The Understanding You Want

Chapter Highlights

The advice to focus on the positive can have a helpful impact in healthy marriages, but this does not mean that we shouldn't address the things that are bothering us. When couples communicate honestly about what is bothering them, this can become an opportunity to turn conflict into connection.

Some Christian resources teach women not to confront their husbands about marriage problems, which can build bad habits over time because small problems aren't corrected early. The Bible's label for Eve, *ezer kenegdo*, means "helper suitable," which is *not* a subordinate role. Being a team means both partners must be able to bring up concerns. This chapter provides different strategies for small concerns and large ones.

It isn't helpful when one spouse keeps quiet about a problem in order to maintain the relationship. By not saying anything, they can enable the other person to avoid making a needed change. When couples focus on keeping a façade of peace in their relationship, they might not ask for what they want directly in order to avoid rejection. Keeping quiet about a problem for a long time can lead to an eventual blowup. This can trigger a fight, flight, freeze, or fawn response in our spouse because they feel threatened.

Instead, frame the issue as a problem to solve together—the other person isn't the problem, the issue is. Consider what is at the root of your disagreement. Sometimes the thing triggering the argument may not be the root issue. Ask "why" until you get to the root of the problem (this may take five times of asking why!).

If someone is causing a problem in the relationship, that person should bear the discomfort of it rather than their spouse. Setting boundaries about what you will and won't do when your spouse does something to harm the relationship is often wise and necessary, but some people find this difficult. If you are afraid to set boundaries or bring up issues in your marriage because of what your spouse might do, that is a red flag for a possibly abusive relationship.

After a conflict, one or both partners need to initiate repair. When one person consistently is the one who initiates repair, marital trust and satisfaction suffer. Small hurts in a marriage can be healed with simple repair, but big harms require a robust repair process, including clear repentance and rebuilding trust over an appropriate period of time. In cases of abuse and betrayal, separation and divorce may be necessary parts of the healing process. A betrayal is what breaks the marriage covenant, not the divorce that results from the betrayal.

Openly dealing with small conflicts early in marriage can prevent some bigger issues from forming later.

Learning Goal

At the end of this lesson, both spouses should feel comfortable confronting issues in their marriage and initiating repair. Each person should also be aware of red flags for abusive behavior.

> When you're asking questions
> that get at what you both emotionally need,
> you're better able to come up with solutions
> you may not have thought of.

Self-Soothing Skill: Self-Compassion

People who cultivate compassion toward themselves have a better overall sense of well-being. Everyone makes mistakes. When someone does something wrong or hurts someone they love, they might tend toward having a self-critical response—an inner voice that beats them up for the infraction. As discussed in the last Self-Soothing Skill on Parts Work, this critical part is trying to protect the person, but the inner criticism can still be distressing. Developing self-compassion instead of self-criticism can bring a sense of inner peace.

Compassion is an emotion of care and concern for someone who is struggling. This emotion motivates action to help the other with their struggle. Consider the parable of the good Samaritan in Luke 10:25-37. Jesus describes the good Samaritan as being moved with compassion for the man injured on the roadside (v. 33). Jesus is also described as compassionate. (See, for example, Matt. 14:14; Mark 1:40-41; Luke 7:13.)

Developing this emotional response to yourself is as important as developing it toward other people. As people learn to be more compassionate to themselves, they will often find that their compassion extends more to others as well. Self-compassion involves self-kindness, a sense of common humanity, and mindfulness. To develop these aspects, consider the following self-talk the next time you feel a self-critical reaction.

Self-kindness: How can I be understanding to myself right now? What is the kindest thing I can do for myself in this moment?

Common humanity: What I am going through is similar to what other humans experience. I am not alone in the world. How would I react toward a child I love who is going through what I'm experiencing? How can I turn that love toward myself?

Mindfulness: What painful thoughts and feelings am I aware of in myself? Can I sit with these sensations a little longer? What can I do to care for myself?

Ideas from: Ulli Zessin, Oliver Dickhäuser, and Sven Garbade, "The Relationship between Self-Compassion and Well-Being: A Meta-Analysis," *Applied Psychology: Health and Well-Being* 7, no. 3 (2015): 340-64.

Questions for Study and Reflection

How can believing the best about your spouse work well in a healthy marriage but cause problems in a troubled marriage?

What does it mean to be emotionally connected to your spouse?

How can we best understand the Hebrew phrase *ezer kenegdo* from Genesis?

What are some practical strategies spouses can use to bring up issues that bother them in marriage?

Why does an imbalance in initiating repair negatively impact a marriage?

Questions for Discussion

Married Couples

Recall a time in your marriage when your spouse confronted you about an issue that bothered them. How did you respond? How was their input helpful to spur you toward growth?

Her answer: _____

His answer: _____

Do you tend to communicate directly or indirectly? How has this impacted your marriage?

Her answer: _____

His answer: _____

Have either of you felt unable to bring up issues in your marriage?

Her answer: _____

His answer: _____

If one of you answered yes: Why do you hesitate to openly address issues? Is this because of teaching that encouraged you to stay silent and submissive? Have your spouse's reactions made you afraid to address issues? Or is there another reason?

Her answer: _____

His answer: _____

When you have felt attacked by your spouse over an issue, what is your typical response? (Circle one or two.)

Her answer: Fight   Flight   Freeze   Fawn

His answer: Fight   Flight   Freeze   Fawn

Which of the following tactics to address issues do you want to try as you begin discussing problem areas in this lesson? (Circle the ones you want to try first.)

Speak openly to your spouse about the issue.

See the issue as a problem to solve together.

Write down the issue on paper to clearly articulate it.

Try to express the other person's point of view to ensure you understand each other's perspectives.

Identify the real issues underneath the initially expressed issue.

Finding the root cause by asking "why?"

Make a list of three issues that feel pressing for you. What do you wish your spouse would do differently?

Her answer:

His answer:

_____

_____

_____

Each of you choose one issue from your spouse's list. Take turns addressing the issue using one or more of the strategies from the list above. In the discussion, make sure not to paint the spouse bringing up the issue as the problem.

When you are done, write a short summary of your resolution here:

If these issues are not resolved within a reasonable timeframe, what boundaries will you set to guide your own behavior? (Look back at the examples of boundaries in the chapter.)

Her answer: _____

His answer: _____

Which one of you usually initiates repair?

Her answer: _____

His answer: _____

If one of you brings up something that has harmed you in your marriage, the one who has done the harming can take this chance to initiate repair, including repentance if necessary.

If the harm was major, check the repair steps from the chapter and commit to following them: "The offender must admit what they have done; admit the depth of the hurt they have caused; make plans to heal that rift; and then follow through before trust can properly be rebuilt."

Does something need to change in your relationship for you both to feel emotionally safe and close to each other? If so, what would that look like?

Her answer: _____

His answer: _____

Premarried Couples

What conflicts have you had so far in your relationship?

Her answer: _____

His answer: _____

How did you resolve these conflicts, or do they remain unresolved?

Her answer: _____

His answer: _____

What skills in addressing issues and resolving conflicts do you want to grow in before you get married?

Her answer: _____

His answer: _____

How do you plan to address issues that will come up once you are married?

Her answer: _____

His answer: _____

How close do you feel emotionally to your partner now? How will you maintain that closeness after you're married?

Her answer: _____

His answer: _____

What are examples of behaviors that are unacceptable in a marriage relationship? What boundaries will you put in place once you're married if your future spouse crosses those lines?

Her answer: _____

His answer: _____

Do you currently see any red flags for abusive behavior in each other?

Her answer: _____

His answer: _____

If so, take some time to reconsider whether marriage at this time is the healthiest choice for both of you. The patterns your partner has now will not change after marriage unless they put in significant work to grow.

> **A boundary isn't about controlling the other person; it is merely stating what you are and are not willing to do.**

Journal Prompt

Make a list of the most important issues you would address with your partner if you could. Choose one to journal about, trying to understand from their perspective why they do what they do. If you feel comfortable, share your thoughts with them and ask if you have understood them correctly.

Prayer Activity

Pray together to confess and repent for ways you have hurt your spouse. Own and focus on your own behavior, not taking any more or less responsibility than you should. Be careful that this does not turn into DARVO, where the abusive partner claims to be the victim or tries to make both of you guilty for a one-sided issue.

Date Idea

Grab some paper and pens and go to your favorite place—for example, a coffee shop or a local park. Make a list of ten ways your spouse can make you feel loved. The rules: They have to be quick (five minutes or less), they have to be nonsexual, and they have to be cheap. Examples might be: greet me when I come in the door; rub my shoulders; buy me a coffee or treat on your way home from work. Share your lists with each other, and each do one of them tonight. Make a conscious effort to do one or two a week from this point on.

Small Group Discussion Questions

1. What are ways that groups can become safe places to discuss hard issues?

2. How would you approach a small issue differently than a big issue in your marriage? When does a small issue become a big issue?

3. What is the silliest issue you have had a fight over in your marriage? What did you learn during the resolution process?

4. Discuss the concept of boundaries. What are some examples of setting boundaries in marriage that are healthy?

5. Why do we sometimes have trouble setting boundaries? How can this group support each other in setting healthy boundaries—in our marriages but also in other relationships we have?

6. Read together Proverbs 27:17 and Hebrews 10:24. How do these Scriptures inspire you toward teamwork in your marriage?

7. What needs to change in your marriage to make it an environment where you can both help each other become more Christlike?

8. When have you changed something about your behavior in response to your spouse's request? How did that impact your marriage?

Key Takeaways

-

-

-

-

Action Items

Her answer:

-

-

-

His answer:

-

-

-

CHAPTER EIGHT

The Closeness You Want

Chapter Highlights

Intimacy in marriage includes sharing your emotions and inner world and listening to your partner do the same. John Powell identifies five levels of communication: cliché, facts, opinions, feelings, and vulnerability. The level of communication with your spouse is a reflection of the intimacy of your relationship. Getting to levels 4 and 5 (feelings and vulnerability) only happens in a few relationships in our lives—and it should happen with our spouses!

Some people are uncomfortable with emotional connection, so they withdraw, or explode, or turn to substances for soothing when uncomfortable emotions are triggered. This can cause pain in their close relationships, especially with their spouses.

Emotions are cognitive constructions based on our past experiences, the current moment including our body sensations, and our future predictions. Even if we have the facts of a situation wrong and our thoughts about those details lead to emotions, those emotions are telling us true things about our values and perspective. Emotions are not bad, and they are not untrustworthy. The Bible describes God as emotional, and humans are made in God's image, emotions and all.

Men and women are equally capable of emotional health. The Bible is full of examples of emotionally expressive men, including Jesus. Both men and women can learn to communicate their emotions. Both men and women can learn to connect in vulnerable ways other than sex.

Couples can build emotional connection by sharing their highs and lows of the day, by practicing naming their emotions, and by asking questions to draw out what the other person felt. Sharing your life stories with each other is another way to deeply connect, including sharing about formative emotional experiences.

If you were not taught as a child how to regulate and process your emotions, you can still learn the skill as an adult. Spouses can learn together how to handle their emotions.

Having your spouse be the witness to your life can create the meaningful marriage you want.

Learning Goal

At the end of this lesson, both spouses should understand emotions better as well as the important role emotional connection plays in a healthy marriage. They should be equipped with strategies to grow their emotional intelligence.

Self-Soothing Skill: Emotional Granularity

Men's minds and women's minds construct emotion in the same way. In Western cultures, women tend to be socialized to pay more attention to their emotions, name them, and share them with others more than men are, but men are equally capable of learning to name, manage, and express their emotions.

According to the theory of constructed emotion from psychologist and neuroscience researcher Lisa Feldman Barrett, emotions are concepts that are constructed in a person's brain based on their *interoception* (sense of what is going on in their body), memory of similar experiences, vocabulary they have been taught about emotions over a lifetime, and the prediction function of the brain about what is likely to happen next and which emotion concept would best fit the circumstance. This name-assigning and meaning-making process in the mind prepares the body to take action to protect the person, to balance the body's energy needs, and to align with the person's values and goals.

Emotional granularity is the ability to be specific in describing how you feel. For example, instead of saying you feel *"bad,"* a greater level of granularity would be to distinguish between feeling angry or sad. If you are angry, a further level of granularity would be to decide if you feel furious, enraged, incensed, frustrated, or annoyed. People who can name and explain their emotions in precise words are more emotionally healthy.

While childhood is a primary time for learning emotion concepts, adults can still learn new and different emotions. Here are some ideas to try to develop your emotional vocabulary:

Google "emotional wheel." There are many different options—look at several of them! They start with a few basic emotions in the center then branch out to further levels of specificity and nuance.

Check out the free app How We Feel, which has an interactive chart for picking the emotion that best fits how you feel and lets you journal about it.

Learn emotion words in other languages. Historian Tiffany Watt Smith wrote a delightful book called *The Book of Human Emotions* that introduces and explains words used in different cultures to describe emotions.

When you feel reactive or unsettled, practice noticing what you feel in your body, what caused the reaction, and what emotion word you want to assign to your experience.

Ideas from: Lisa Feldman Barrett, *How Emotions Are Made* (Boston: Mariner, 2017); and Christine D. Wilson-Mendenhall and John D. Dunne, "Cultivating Emotional Granularity," *Frontiers in Psychology* 12 (November 2021), https://doi.org/10.3389/fpsyg.2021.703658.

True intimacy requires vulnerability.
We must have courage to share what's
on our hearts, and we must provide safety
so that our spouse can do the same.

Questions for Study and Reflection

What are the five levels of communication according to John Powell?

Why do some people avoid communication at levels 4 and 5?

What are the two ingredients for connection mentioned in this chapter?

Define *emotion* in your own words based on this chapter.

What are some biblical examples of healthy emotional expression—both pleasant and unpleasant?

Questions for Discussion

Married Couples

Which of the five levels of communication do you spend the most time on in your marriage?

Her answer: _____

His answer: _____

What is the deepest level of communication you reach in your marriage? How often do you get to that level?

Her answer: _____

His answer: _____

How has your level of communication changed over the time you've been married? Has it grown deeper or gotten shallower?

Her answer: _____

His answer: _____

Do you feel safe being vulnerable with your spouse?

Her answer: _____

His answer: _____

How can you create safety for your spouse to be vulnerable with you?

Her answer: _____

His answer: _____

Do either of you have frustrations about your spouse's emotional connection in your relationship?

Her answer: _____

His answer: _____

How did your childhood and past teaching in Christian circles shape what you believe about emotions?

Her answer: _____

His answer: _____

How has your life story impacted your ability to face and name your emotions today?

Her answer: _____

His answer: _____

What would it change for you to see emotions as helpful and important instead of bad or untrustworthy (if this is a problem for you)?

Which emotional connection strategies would you like to try? (Circle the ones you want to do first.)

Emotional recap (highs and lows)

Name emotions

Ask curious questions to find out more

Volunteer insights

Ask about your spouse's emotional backstory

Do you ever feel emotionally flooded when your spouse is angry? How do you want to handle that the next time it happens?

Her answer: _____

His answer: _____

Do you currently feel like your spouse is a witness to your life? If not, what would need to change for that to be true?

Her answer: _____

His answer: _____

Premarried Couples

How did your parents or caregivers model emotional expression in your home?

Her answer: _____

His answer: _____

What do you want emotional expression to look like in your own home together? Do you want to do things similarly to your caregivers or differently?

Her answer: _____

His answer: _____

What is the current level of emotional connection in your relationship? (1 is not at all connected emotionally, and 10 is highly connected emotionally.)

Her answer:

1   2   3   4   5   6   7   8   9   10

His answer:

1   2   3   4   5   6   7   8   9   10

Are you happy with the levels of communication (1–5) that you currently speak at in your relationship?

Her answer: _____

His answer: _____

Have you had any opportunities to mourn together in your relationship so far? How supported did you feel?

Her answer: _____

His answer: _____

What would you like to see grow in your vulnerability and trust as you move closer to marriage?

Her answer: _____

His answer: _____

Tell your partner about a past experience that still impacts your life today.

Her answer: _____

His answer: _____

Journal Prompt

Think about a recent time when you felt a strong emotional reaction. Go through the four "Questions to Help Examine Your Emotions" (from the sidebar in chap. 8 of *The Marriage You Want*) and journal your answers:

What is my body feeling right now?

What am I preoccupied with right now?

How am I painting myself right now?

What story am I narrating to myself right now?

When you finish, consider what you understand about that emotional reaction now better than you did before you sat down to journal. What name would you give this emotion? Why did you construct that emotion?

Prayer Activity

Ask God to make you emotional like Jesus is emotional. Thank God for the good gift of emotions, which are a part of being made in God's image.

Date Idea

Plan a date to a place that holds nostalgia or emotional significance to one of you, if possible, a place that reminds you of your younger years. While on your date, tell stories about your life growing up that your spouse hasn't heard before.

Small Group Discussion Questions

1. Consider the conversation level of this group. Have we gotten to levels 4 and 5? If yes, share what helped us get there.
2. What gender-based stereotypes do you have around emotions?
3. List pop culture references that have reinforced gendered stereotypes of emotions.
4. Now list pop culture references of examples that go against gendered emotion stereotypes.
5. What is the worst advice you've ever gotten about emotions?
6. What is the best emotion advice you have ever received?
7. List as many of Jesus' emotions as you can. (Googling is okay!) What do you notice about Jesus' emotions?
8. Name an emotion you constructed today. What led to that emotional reaction from you? Other group members can ask questions to flesh out the experience.
9. As we conclude this study together, what has been the most impactful thing you learned?
10. How do you want to do marriage differently after this study?

Key Takeaways

-
-
-
-

Action Items

Her answer:

-
-
-

His answer:

-
-
-

> There is nothing about being a man
> that means he can't be emotionally healthy
> and nothing about being a woman
> that means she automatically will be.

Sheila Wray Gregoire is the face behind BareMarriage  .com as well as a sought-after speaker and the award-winning author or coauthor of nine books, including *The Great Sex Rescue* and *She Deserves Better*. With her humorous, no-nonsense approach, Sheila is passionate about changing the evangelical conversation about sex and marriage to make it healthy, evidence-based, and biblical. She and her husband, Keith, live in Ontario, Canada, near their two adult daughters and three grandchildren. Sheila also knits. Even in line at the grocery store.

Dr. Keith Gregoire is a physician and the coauthor  with Sheila of *The Good Guy's Guide to Great Sex*, companion to her award-winning *The Good Girl's Guide to Great Sex*. Currently, Keith spends most of his professional time providing pediatric care to remote communities in northern Ontario. Plus he birdwatches. Even during mosquito season.

Connect with Sheila and Keith:

BareMarriage.com

 BareMarriageOfficial   SheilaGregoire   SheilaGregoire

Listen to the *Bare Marriage* podcast every Thursday!

Becky Castle Miller is working on a PhD in New Testament at Wheaton College, writing a dissertation on emotions in the Gospel of Luke. She graduated from Northern Seminary. She and her husband, Matthew, have been married for over twenty years and have five children. They returned to the United States in 2020 after eight years of serving at an international church in the Netherlands. She is coauthor of the discipleship workbook *Following King Jesus* with Scot McKnight.